The Craft of Writing

of Writing

Marshall Cavendish
Benchmark
New York

Fiction

DAN ELISH

Other Marshall Cavendish Offices:
Marshall Cavendish International (Asia) Private Limited, 1 New Industrial Road, Singapore 536196 • Marshall Cavendish International (Thailand) Co Ltd. 253 Asoke, 12th Flr, Sukhumvit 21 Road, Klongtoey Nua, Wattana, Bangkok 10110, Thailand • Marshall Cavendish (Malaysia) Sdn Bhd, Times Subang, Lot 46, Subang Hi-Tech Industrial Park, Batu Tiga, 40000 Shah Alam, Selangor Darul Ehsan, Malaysia

Marshall Cavendish is a trademark of Times Publishing Limited.

All websites were available and accurate when this book was sent to press.

Library of Congress Cataloging-in-Publication Data

Elish, Dan. • Fiction / Dan Elish. • p. cm.— (The craft of writing)
Includes bibliographical references and index. • ISBN 978-1-60870-497-2 (print)
ISBN 978-1-60870-649-5 (ebook) • 1. Fiction—Authorship. 2. Fiction—Technique.
I. Title. • PN3355.E55 2012 • 808.3—dc22 • 2010018776

Publisher: Michelle Bisson • Art Director: Anahid Hamparian
Series Designer: Alicia Mikles • Photo research by Lindsay Aveilhe

The photographs in this book with permission and through courtesy of:
iStockphoto: cover; iStockphoto: 2; Imagezoo/Images.com/Getty Images: 4; Getty Images: 9; Buyenlarge/Getty Images: 10; Alex Bailey/Focus Features/Studi/Bureau L.A. Collection/Corbis: 13; Stapleton Historical Collection/HIP/The Image Works: 21; Kobal Collection: 22; Photos 12/Alamy: 26; Everett Collection: 29; Reuters/Corbis: 31; Warner Bros./Peter Mountain/The Kobal Collection: 34; Banew Line Cinema/Pierre Vinet/The Kobal Collection: 37; Age fotostock/SuperStock: 42; Sion Touhig/Sygma/Corbis: 44; Mary Evans/Ronald Grant/Everett Collection: 47; John Springer Collection/Corbis: 50; The Granger Collection: 59; Tom and Steve/Getty Images: 64; Bob Daemmrich/PhotoEdit: 77; Todd Davidson/Getty Images: 80.

Printed in Malaysia (T)
135642

Contents

Introduction

WHAT IS THIS THING called fiction? Simply put, a work of fiction is a story told in prose. Most often, these stories are dished out in two different forms: the short story and the novel.

A short story is pretty much what it sounds like—a story on the short side that focuses on a single character, dramatic event, or theme. Often, there's not much action in a short story; the author is usually more interested in subtle psychological shifts in his or her characters.

In a novel, on the other hand, the writer paints on a broader canvas; there is more character development, and the story is longer and fuller. In terms of subject matter, anything goes. There have been novels written about everything from the Vietnam War to a boy lost at sea with a raft full of animals, including an orangutan, a zebra, a hyena, and a tiger. J. K. Rowling's best-selling Harry Potter novels are about the trials and tribulations of a boy wizard.

Fiction

How do these novels and short stories get written? Who are these strange people called writers? Brenda Ueland, best known for her book *If You Want to Write*, once said, "Everybody is talented, original and has something important to say." In other words, there is a writer in everyone. Not that writing is necessarily easy. Like anything, it takes discipline and hard work to learn to write well. If you have ever leafed through a novel in your local Barnes & Noble and thought, "I could NEVER do that!" this book is here to tell you that you can. Generations of authors have felt overwhelmed at the thought of facing a blank page. But then they sat down and got to work.

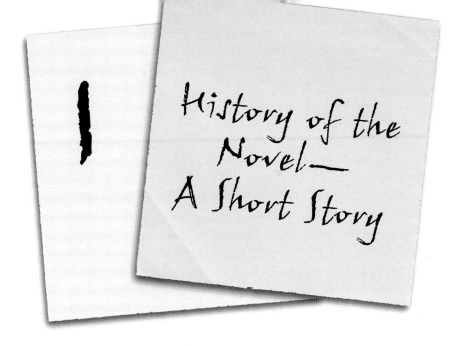

History of the
Novel—
A Short Story

SINCE PREHISTORIC HUMANS drew pictures on cave walls, people have told stories. In ancient Greece, Homer wrote the *Iliad*, an epic poem recounting the drama and glory of the Trojan War. In the eleventh century, Marco Polo dictated the stories of his exotic travels to a prison cell mate. Storytelling in the Middle Ages was, by necessity, an oral, or spoken, tradition. Multiple copies of a single story had to be written down by hand or sometimes engraved in wood and then inked and pressed onto a sheet of paper, tasks that were enormously time consuming. The mass production of books became possible in 1440 when a German inventor, Johannes Gutenberg, invented a printing press that used movable type and oil-based inks. Around 1454, Gutenberg produced an edition of the Bible, arguably the first widely published book.

But what of the novel? Did Gutenberg's invention send hordes of would-be storytellers to their rooms to get working? The answer is no. The novel as we know it today—a long story in prose about a set of characters who go on some sort of adventure that usually leads to some sort of emotional growth—took a few hundred more years to come about.

Early Novels

By the seventeenth century, plenty of good novels were being penned across Europe. One of the most notable contributions was *Don Quixote*, by the Spanish writer Miguel de Cervantes. Published in two parts (Part 1, 1605; Part 2, 1615), *Don Quixote* is a comic novel about a middle-aged man who leaves his home, takes up a sword, and travels the countryside to protect the innocent and defeat the wicked.

Despite the success of *Don Quixote*, the development of the novel took place largely in England. From 1649 until 1660, Britain was ruled by the Puritan Commonwealth, a government with strict religious laws. The restoration of the monarchy in 1660, however, encouraged the creation of secular (that is, nonreligious) storytelling. Newspapers were founded. Political and philosophical ideas were openly debated. With increased leisure time for the middle class, people suddenly had more time to read—and write.

In 1719 an adventure story titled *Robinson Crusoe*, by the English author and journalist Daniel Defoe, was published. In molding his famous work, Defoe made use of the picaresque style, which derived from Spain. Pica-

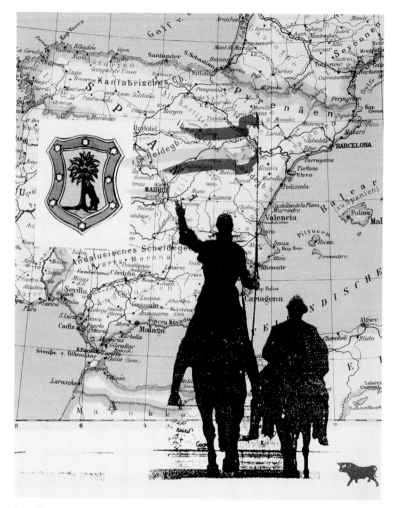

Don Quixote and his faithful sidekick Sancho Panza set off on a journey to see the world that has remained a favorite of fiction lovers for centuries.

resque stories usually concern the adventures of a rogue (a dishonest man). *Robinson Crusoe* tells the adventures of an English castaway who spends twenty-eight years on a tropical island before finally being rescued.

The Full Title

Defoe's novel was first published in 1719
with the title:

The Life and strange Surprizing Adventures
of Robinson Crusoe of York, Mariner: Who
lived Eight and Twenty Years, all alone
in an un-inhabited Island on the coast of
America, near the Mouth of the Great River
of Oroonoque; Having been cast on Shore
by Shipwreck, where-in all the Men perished
but himself. With An Account how he was
at last as strangely deliver'd by Pyrates.
Written by Himself.

This illustration of Robinson Crusoe on his raft was created
around 1900 by Newell Convers Wyeth, an American artist who
created artwork for more than three thousand books.

Other Early Novels

Most scholars agree that the next important novelist was Henry Fielding. A lawyer and the founder of what some call London's first police force, the Bow Street Runners, Fielding was also a satiric playwright and the author of two very popular picaresque novels, *Joseph Andrews* (1742) and *Tom Jones* (1746), each telling the story of a lovable, comic rogue.

What set Fielding apart in the development of the novel was not so much his stories as his approach toward the art of fiction. Writers before Fielding presented their stories as though they had actually happened. For example, Defoe wrote *Robinson Crusoe* as a memoir, a man's written remembrances of something he had actually experienced. Readers nowadays take it for granted that the story comes entirely out of the author's imagination. Fielding was the first major writer to make no bones about the fact that he was making it all up.

A decade after Fielding published his two best-known works, writer Laurence Sterne, who was also a clergyman, wrote *Tristram Shandy*, the longest, most ambitious early novel. Bearing the full title *The Life and Opinions of Tristram Shandy, Gentleman*, the book appeared in nine volumes of roughly two hundred pages each. Despite its length, readers delighted in its bawdy humor and Sterne's willingness to poke fun at the London aristocracy. *Shandy* also stretched the definition of what a novel could do. Most authors stick carefully to their story line, but Sterne gave himself the freedom to go off on wild tangents about whatever interested him along the way. In fact, *Tristram*

Shandy is so full of digressions that the main character does not even appear until the third volume. Clearly, Sterne felt that a writer should be free to shoot from the hip and comment on anything he wanted.

The Novel of Manners

Jane Austen introduced what is now called the "novel of manners." This early-nineteenth-century author's works used humor to shed light on some of the idiocies of the social conventions of the time. Her most famous work, *Pride and Prejudice* (published in 1813) begins, "It is a

Though *Pride and Prejudice* was written in the early nineteenth century, it may well be even more popular today. In the past few years, countless spinoffs have been published and several film versions of the story have been produced.

truth universally acknowledged, that a single man in possession of a good fortune must be in want of a wife." For the next three hundred pages the reader has the good fortune of watching the oldest Bennet sister, Jane, eventually marry the rich Mr. Bingley despite their difference in social class, while her younger sister, the outspoken Lizzy, falls in and out of love with the arrogant Mr. Darcy. That, too, has a happy ending.

While Austen's books are comic, they highlight the plight of the women of her time, who depended upon a good marriage to achieve social standing and financial security. Women at that time had no financial rights and no opportunities for careers. Because she chose to publish her works anonymously, Austen's novels brought her little fame during her lifetime. But *A Memoir of Jane Austen*, written by her nephew, led to a wider readership. Today she is respected as one of history's great novelists.

Charles Dickens and the Novel of Social Justice

Most young readers today know the work of Charles Dickens. *Oliver Twist* is the tale of a poor orphan who joins a gang of London pickpockets. *A Christmas Carol* is the story of the miserly Scrooge and his encounters with the ghosts of Christmas past, present, and future. Dickens's opening lines of *A Tale of Two Cities* are among the most famous in all literature: "It was the best of times, it was the worst of times."

The Brilliant Brontës

Charlotte, Emily, and Anne Brontë were raised in West Yorkshire, England, and each grew up to become a famous novelist whose works are still read widely. Charlotte's *Jane Eyre* tells the story of a determined, often mistreated orphan who eventually finds happiness. Emily's *Wuthering Heights*, one of the most wrenching love stories in literature, tells the tale of the tortured love between Catherine Earnshaw and her mistreated stepbrother, Heathcliff. Anne's *Agnes Grey* tells the tale of a woman who is forced to become a governess. All three novels were published in 1847. Today *Jane Eyre* and *Wuthering Heights* are considered two of the best examples of the nineteenth-century novel.

Born in 1812, Dickens created book after book with sharply written, memorable characters and well-honed plots. Enormously popular in his day, his novels were not published as finished works but were serialized monthly in magazines. Writing to meet deadline after deadline, Dickens's work developed a particular rhythm. Each chapter ended with a cliffhanger that left the reader eager to buy the next installment.

But Dickens was more than just a talented entertainer. He was one of the first authors to use his writing to draw attention to injustice. Who can forget Oliver Twist asking the master of the workhouse if he can "please have some more"? Or Tiny Tim, the crippled son of Bob Cratchit, saying, "God Bless us, everyone"? Harriet Martineau, a literary critic at that time, said, "It is scarcely conceivable that anyone should . . . exert a stronger social influence than Mr. Dickens has. . . . His sympathies are on the side of the suffering and the frail; and this makes him the idol of those who suffer, from whatever cause."

Dickens's novels often deal with the adventures and misfortunes of children. It was the subject that interested him most as a writer. He once said, "A boy's story is the best that is ever told."

The Great Russian Writers

No discussion of the development of the novel could be complete without mention of two great Russian novelists. Some critics have heralded Fyodor Dostoyevsky as the

The Greatest Novel of Them All?

Mary Ann (sometimes spelled Mary Anne or Marian) Evans was born on November 22, 1819, but was better known by her pen name, George Eliot. One of the leading writers of the Victorian era, her books are prized for their realism and psychological insight. Her best, published in 1872, is *Middlemarch*, a novel that many scholars consider to be one of the finest ever written. The British writer and critic V. S. Pritchett wrote,

> "No Victorian novel approaches *Middlemarch* in its width of reference, its intellectual power, or the imperturbable spaciousness of its narrative. . . . I doubt if any Victorian novelist has as much to teach the modern novelists as George Eliot . . ."

writer with the most exceptional psychological insight into his characters. Born in 1821, Dostoyevsky studied mathematics in college and then joined the army before becoming a writer. His best-known novel, *Crime and Punishment*, tells the story of a poor student, Rodion Romanovich Raskolnikov, who sets out to kill a greedy pawnbroker for her money but botches the murder and kills her half sister as well. For the rest of the book, Dostoyevsky explores Raskolnikov's psychological state as he wrestles with his crime and eventually turns himself in to the police.

The other major Russian novelist was Leo Tolstoy. Born into a family of the Russian nobility, Tolstoy spent his career writing fiction that was often sharply critical of the upper classes. His most famous novel, *War and Peace*, uses a large, brilliantly developed cast of characters to examine the nature of war and the reactions to it of a cross section of Russian aristocratic society—people whose modes of living, attitudes, virtues, and defects are far from uniform. His other widely studied novel, *Anna Karenina*, is considered a masterpiece of realistic fiction. It tells the tale of a woman's downward psychological spiral, a fall that ends only with her suicide. Tolstoy's countryman and fellow writer Dostoyevsky called *Anna Karenina* "a flawless work of art."

American Literature

The art of the novel soon made its way from Europe across the Atlantic Ocean to the United States. In the mid–1800s

James Joyce

Known as the first modernist, James Joyce was an Irish writer who took the novel in new directions, writing in a style known as stream of consciousness, in which a given character's thoughts flow without close regard to conventional plot. His masterpiece, *Ulysses*, which takes place in a single day, June 16, 1904, sets the story of Homer's *Odyssey* in Dublin, Ireland. Though it is very difficult to read, *Ulysses* is considered by many scholars to be one of the twentieth century's greatest novels.

Fiction

Nathaniel Hawthorne wrote *The Scarlet Letter*, the quintessential novel of life in Puritan New England. Herman Melville's *Moby Dick* is a great adventure story as well as a complex rumination on man and nature. Henry James wrote some of America's most psychologically complex novels, notably *The Ambassadors*.

But many scholars would agree that American literature began in earnest in 1884 with the publication of Mark Twain's *The Adventures of Huckleberry Finn*. Narrated by Huck, a young teen, Twain's novel was the first to use the American vernacular to tell a story. Readers of today have experience with ungrammatical first-person narrators, but the opening lines of *Huckleberry Finn* were an innovation in the late nineteenth century: "You don't know about me, without you have read a book by the name of *The Adventures of Tom Sawyer*, but that ain't no matter." Possessing an energy and spirit about it that were uniquely American, scholars point to *Huckleberry Finn* as one of the most important American novels.

The twentieth century saw a flowering of great American writers. Three stand out for their influence and excellence. Born in 1899 in Oak Park, Illinois, Ernest Hemingway brought a remarkable realism to his work. Known for books such as *The Sun Also Rises* and *A Farewell to Arms*, Hemingway developed a signature style that was sparse and direct.

Another great American writer of the twentieth century was Midwestern native F. Scott Fitzgerald. His first novel, *This Side of Paradise*, about Amory Blaine, a student

Mark Twain, dressed in his signature white suit even when playing pool, is believed by many scholars to be the first truly American novelist.

at Princeton University, made him an overnight celebrity. His masterpiece, *The Great Gatsby*, is the story of a man's pursuit of the woman he loves, and through her, of the American dream of wealth and happiness. It has come to be thought of as one of the great novels of the century. Employing a style as poetic as Hemingway's was simple, Fitzgerald wrote of the American experience with a beauty that may still be unmatched in American literature.

Readers of *The Great Gatsby* would instantly recognize this scene as one of the lavish parties Jay Gatsby threw in the hope of luring back his lost love, Daisy.

From The *Great Gatsby*

"Most of the big shore places were closed now and there were hardly any lights except the shadowy, moving glow of a ferryboat across the Sound. And as the moon rose higher the inessential houses began to melt away until gradually I became aware of the old island here that flowered once for Dutch sailors' eyes—a fresh, green breast of the new world. Its vanished trees, the trees that had made way for Gatsby's house, had once pandered in whispers to the last and greatest of all human dreams; for a transitory enchanted moment man must have held his breath in the presence of this continent, compelled into an aesthetic contemplation he neither understood nor desired, face to face for the last time in history with something commensurate to his capacity for wonder."

—F. Scott Fitzgerald

Finally, there is William Faulkner. A Mississippian, he set his many novels in a fictional southern county, creating a stunning portrait of former slaves and poor white farmers. Where Hemingway made his mark with a self-consciously direct style and Fitzgerald with a more poetic one, Faulkner made use of stream of consciousness. His books are more difficult to comprehend—and may be best experienced for the first time with the help of a teacher—but Faulkner's work is unique in the depth of his portrayal of his characters and of the American South.

Short Fiction

While many writers prefer the longer form of the novel, others feel they can better express themselves in a shorter form. The earliest short stories were fables—tales with a moral. The most famous fables are those of Aesop, a Greek slave. Much later, in fourteenth-century Europe, stories that had been passed down orally through the generations began to be written down, most notably Geoffrey Chaucer's *Canterbury Tales*.

In the mid–1820s in Germany, the Brothers Grimm published their now-famous fairy tales. At the same time in America, Washington Irving wrote "The Legend of Sleepy Hollow," featuring Rip Van Winkle. Two decades later, Edgar Allan Poe began writing his tales of horror, among them "The Tell-Tale Heart." In the late 1800s, the Russian writer Anton Chekhov penned some of the most powerful short fiction ever written.

More recent practitioners of the art include John Updike, who wrote realistic stories of life in America's suburbs, Raymond Carver, who wrote movingly about people who often lack a voice, and Lorrie Moore, known for her sharp wit and refreshing insights into modern life.

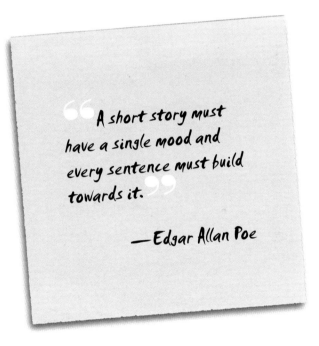

" A short story must have a single mood and every sentence must build towards it. "

—Edgar Allan Poe

Fiction Today

Today the art of fiction is thriving. Despite the influence of television and the Internet, more people are trying to write short stories and novels than ever before. In the early years of the twenty-first century, fiction has come to be virtually anything—from Jonathan Franzen's *Freedom*, an

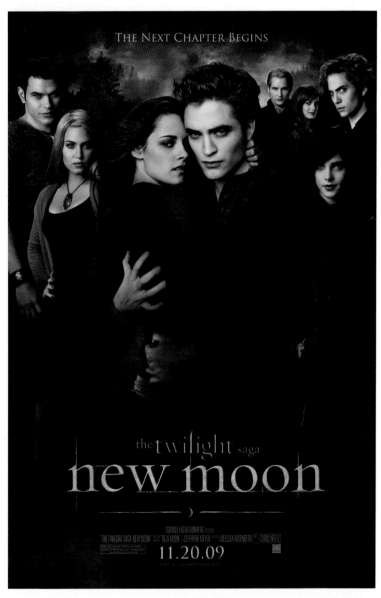

Stephenie Meyer's best selling series *Twilight* is delighting and inspiring a whole new generation of readers.

exploration of the American family, to *Interpreter of Maladies*, the short story collection by the Indian American Jhumpa Lahiri that won the Pulitzer Prize in 2000, to Stephenie Meyer's best-selling series *Twilight*, which deals with the life and times of teen vampires. Genres abound: mysteries, romances, detective stories, political thrillers, young-adult novels, and of course, short stories. Anything and everything is up for grabs. Modern-day writers have three centuries of great works to be inspired by. Everyone should be encouraged to try. The American historian and author Richard Rhodes put it best:

> **If you want to be a writer, you can. Fear stops most people from writing, not lack of talent, whatever that is. . . . You're a human being with a unique story to tell. . . . If you speak with passion, many of us will listen. We need stories to live, all of us. We live by story. Yours enlarges the circle.**

2

The Big
Picture

SO YOU HAVE DECIDED you want to write something, a short story or maybe even a novel. You might even have a specific story in mind, something you're itching to get down on paper. But the whole process seems too big, too intimidating. How do you get started?

Remember, fiction writing is an art, not a science. There is no absolute right way of doing it. Still, most successful stories do have certain attributes in common.

The opening chapter of this book concerned the history of fiction. The remaining four chapters offer advice on things that you, the young author, can think about while crafting your first stories.

The Main Character

What is the first thing a writer should think about when getting started on a book?

The Adventures of Huckleberry Finn is a novel told through the eyes and voice of Huck Finn, a device that makes the story far more powerful than if it had been told by a distant, or even adult, narrator.

Again, everyone is different, but until a writer has a handle on the main character, getting started is going to be tough. Think about it. Most novels focus on one central protagonist (another word for the main character) who has some sort of serious problem to work out. Take Huck Finn, for example, a boy with his share of troubles. As Twain's novel opens, Huck is living with the Widow Douglas, a lady who has set out to "sivilize him," by making him wear "new clothes" and say his prayers. She doesn't even let him smoke! By page three, Huck says he feels so lonesome he wishes he were dead. By the end of chapter one, Twain has set up the book's scenario. Huck wants something desperately: to get away from the widow and live on his own. Soon enough, he fakes his own death and takes off on a raft down the Mississippi River with a slave named Jim.

A more recently created fictional character, the protagonist of a series of books, is Harry Potter, another boy with his share of troubles. At the opening of the Harry Potter series, Harry, an orphan, is living with his very mean Aunt and Uncle Dursley who favor their own obnoxious son and treat Harry horribly. By the end of chapter one, the reader is rooting for Harry to get away as quickly as possible. Soon enough, despite the Dursleys' best efforts, Harry leaves their home and finds his way to Hogwarts, a school for magicians, where he learns the secret of his own real parents.

So, as you think about your story, ask yourself about your main character. Who is it? Where does he or she live? What does he do? Once you know the answers to these questions, ask yourself if the character has a problem to work out. If the answer is yes, you've probably made a good start. The fiction writer Stanley Elkin once observed, "I would never write about someone who is not at the end of his rope."

The Harry Potter series was a phenomenon in young fiction. Fans lined the streets each time a new book in the series went on sale.

Maxwell Perkins

Maxwell Perkins (1884–1947) was one of America's most famous editors. Working at Charles Scribner's Sons in the early to middle part of the twentieth century, Perkins edited such classics as Fitzgerald's *The Great Gatsby*, Hemingway's *The Sun Also Rises*, Thomas Wolfe's *Look Homeward, Angel*, and Marjorie Rawlings's *The Yearling*. Perkins once wrote,

"Writing a novel is a very hard thing to do because it covers so long a space of time, and if you get discouraged it is not a bad sign, but a good one. If you think you are not doing it well, you are thinking the way real novelists do. I never knew one who did not feel greatly discouraged at times, and some get desperate, and I have always found that to be a good symptom."

Something to Want

After you've given your main character some sort of problem, a related question to ask is, "What does my character want?" Once you identify what your main character really desires, you'll be another step along toward figuring out what happens next.

At the beginning of J. D. Salinger's novel *The Catcher in the Rye*, Holden Caulfield is a sixteen-year-old boy who is about to be thrown out of Pencey Prep School. What Holden wants more than anything is to get away from the "phonies" in his school. As a result, he makes his way by himself to New York City, where the main action of the novel takes place.

All compelling stories usually begin with a main character who wants something, regardless of the genre. Another example is Frodo, in J. R. R. Tolkien's *The Lord of the Rings*. As the story begins, Bilbo Baggins, Frodo's uncle and guardian, mysteriously disappears, leaving behind a powerful ring. A great wizard named Gandalf arrives and tells Frodo that the ring is dangerous. With terrifying riders scouring the countryside, Frodo decides to take the ring and run for his life. At this point, Frodo wants many things. He wants to escape the threat of the dark riders and to discover the true meaning of the ring. He also wants to find Bilbo.

Sometimes what a main character wants is very simple. Roald Dahl's children's novel *Charlie and the Chocolate Factory* begins by introducing the reader to Charlie, a boy whose family has practically nothing to eat but happens to live in the same town as the most wonderful chocolate

Fiction

In *Charlie and the Chocolate Factory*, Roald Dahl wrote with such wit, warmth, and attention to detail that he made Willy Wonka's magical factory seem real.

factory in the world. Charlie wants food: namely, chocolate. Soon enough, he finds the final gold ticket that allows him inside Willy Wonka's chocolate factory. Who wouldn't invite a little boy who is so poor that his dad earns a living screwing caps on tubes of toothpaste to get what he wants?

Indeed, once you discover what your main character desires more than anything else in the world, your job will be much easier. Ray Bradbury, one of the best science fiction writers of the twentieth century, put it this way: "Find out what your hero or heroine wants, and when he or she wakes up in the morning, just follow him or her all day."

Keep It Real

The writer Ethan Canin once said, "Nothing is as important as a likable narrator. Nothing holds a story together better." What did Canin mean by "likable"? Does he mean readers have to love the narrator of each book? Does he mean that the main character has to be perfect? Not at all. What Canin is getting at is that stories work better when the reader cares about the protagonist. A likable main character is a character who may not be perfect but is sympathetic.

For example, Huck Finn is a narrator who, if he were alive today, would be thought to have a multitude of faults. He won't go to school, won't wear clean clothes, and he smokes. Also, as was very common in pre-Civil War times, Huck considered Jim inferior to him because he was black and a slave. Yet Huck is one of the most likable narrators ever written because he is funny and completely honest. The reader feels sympathy for him because, despite having a dead mother and a father who is a murderous drunk, Huck never feels sorry for himself.

Well-written main characters have their good points and bad points. Who, after all, wants to read an entire novel about someone who has a great job, is happily married, lives in a gorgeous mansion, and whose only problem is which of his six cars to drive to work each morning.

Fiction

Similarly, it's hard to read about a character who is so horrible that he hates his job, his friends, and his family, and even kicks his dog. The most successful characters are, like all of us, real human beings who have many good qualities but also their share of flaws.

Beginning, Middle, and End

After you get a handle on your main character, what next? Do you sit in front of your computer and start typing? Maybe. However, you might be better off if you sit in front of your computer—or anywhere for that matter— and think about the shape of your story.

Stories need a well-thought-out beginning, middle, and end. There is nothing more frustrating than getting hooked on a book with a fantastic first half, only to discover that the author had no idea whatsoever how to resolve the story. The author who writes a weak opening also risks losing the reader's interest. You don't have to plot out every single detail before you begin, but you should have a general idea of where your story is headed and a few of the stops it will make along the way.

It is clear that even though *The Lord of the Rings* is a long and sprawling work, Tolkien had a pretty good idea of how each chapter would work before he started. I'm sure he knew that the book would start with Frodo and Sam Gamgee running from the Shire with the ring of power. I imagine he also knew that Frodo and Sam would join a fellowship of seven other characters who would be assigned

The Lord of the Rings is over a thousand pages long, but it holds one's interest because J. R. R. Tolkien immerses the reader in a complete world of his own invention.

37

the task of destroying the ring in the land of Mordor. Finally, I feel certain that Tolkien knew how he wanted to end the whole thing. Would Frodo destroy the ring? Or would the ring destroy Frodo?

The beginning of a good story sets up a series of questions for the reader. At the beginning of *The Lord of the Rings*, the reader wonders what will happen to Frodo. What is the ring? Will Frodo even live? Indeed, it is a life-or-death situation. The fate of the entire Middle Earth stands on the shoulders of one young hobbit! The middle of the story takes the main character through a series of logical but surprising events that lead to the final climax or conclusion. In *The Lord of the Rings*, Frodo and the members of the fellowship set off for the land of Mordor. On the way, they encounter everything from dangerous wizards to killer Orcs, but Frodo and Sam manage to push their way to their goal. Finally, the action builds to the grand finale—the part of the book where everything that has come before pays off.

Though *The Lord of the Rings* is over a thousand pages long, the same principles apply to shorter fiction. Even a two-page tale by Hans Christian Andersen starts with a central idea that gets developed and then reaches a final conclusion. Though the action of many short stories may be subtle, a writer needs to supply a basic shape to the story that the reader can hold on to. Shirley Jackson's classic, and much taught, short story "The Lottery" is a good example of a well-crafted story.

The beginning: Jackson, setting the scene, describes

a town with a strange custom. Each year in June, there is some sort of lottery in which a single person in the town is picked.

The middle: families gather and draw straws, and the grisly truth is subtly revealed—the "winner" will be stoned to death by the other townspeople, a tradition that allegedly blesses the annual harvest. The Hutchinson family is picked.

The end: with another drawing, Tessie Hutchinson, the last arrival at the lottery, is chosen. As the story closes, the town gathers to send her to her doom.

"The Lottery" is thought to be one of America's greatest short stories. Though it owes its success to many different elements, one of them is its structure.

Characters' Motivations Move the Plot

By this point, you know several things about your upcoming piece of writing. You know what your main character wants. You have done your best to make him or her a real, living person with good and bad qualities. You have thought a little bit about your beginning, middle, and end. So how do you fill out the rest of the plot? Anne Lamott, a writing teacher and author, offers some advice:

"Plot grows out of character. If you focus on who the people in your story are, if you sit and write about two people you know and are getting to know better day by day, something is bound to happen."

Take a moment and listen to what your main character most desires. Huck Finn wanted to get away from the Widow Douglas. Accordingly, Twain sent him on an adventure up the Mississippi River. In *The Catcher in the Rye*, Holden Caulfield wanted to get away from his classmates. So Salinger sent him to New York City. When Rowling listened to what Harry Potter wanted, she realized that he was a boy desperate to discover his true destiny and the fate of his parents, so she sent him to Hogwarts.

Everyone has read a book where the events become harder and harder to believe. Often, in such a case, what happens in the book does not agree with the set-up of the story or the true nature of the main character. An example

> "I have never demanded of a set of characters that they do things my way. On the contrary, I want them to do things their way."
>
> —Stephen King

might be helpful. A novel entitled *The Tale of Liz*, about a woman who works as a legal assistant in a law firm, begins with a description of Liz as a quiet girl who does not get out much and secretly wants to be an opera star. If the writer develops the story by having Liz quit her job to study opera in Italy, the reader might believe it. However, if the writer suddenly gets nervous that his book is dull and has Liz confess to a friend that she is from the third moon of Neptune and has been hired by Iran to steal America's nuclear codes, the reader probably won't buy it. Events in stories need to make sense. They need to follow from a main character whose desires and characteristics are clearly defined. When something unexpected but unmotivated appears out of nowhere to spice up the action, it can make the reader mistrust the author.

A good piece of advice is to always listen to your characters and let them drive the action. In his book *On Writing*, the famed author of horror fiction Stephen King writes, "I have never demanded of a set of characters that they do things my way. On the contrary, I want them to do things their way."

The Fictional Dream

What happens when the source of the plot's development is a character's deepest desires? The answer, plain and simple, is a story that the reader believes in completely. It doesn't matter if a novel is a realistic work about life in a prison or a fantasy about a flying horse who speaks Mandarin.

Fiction

The successful fiction writer creates an imaginary world for the reader that is as absorbing as our own nightly dreams—but much more memorable.

If you have set up the world of your story honestly, the reader will go along for the ride. However, if, as in *The Story of Liz*, your characters jump from one implausible event to the next, the reader will probably toss the book aside with no regrets.

John Gardner was a well-known novelist and one of the most influential writing teachers of his era. Though he died in 1982, his books on writing are still used in workshops and widely studied today. He wrote that every time a writer puts words on a page, he must create a dream for the reader that is "vivid and continuous." He said, "We read five words on the first page of a really good novel and we begin to forget that we are reading printed words on a page; we begin to see images . . . we slip into a dream, forgetting the room we're sitting in, forgetting it's lunchtime or time to go to work."

When a reader picks up a book, he enters a new world. It is the author's job to make sure that the story is well-conceived and written so that it unfolds clearly in the reader's mind. In the next chapter, you will find some useful tools to help create "vivid and continuous" fictional dreams.

J. K. Rowling chose to tell the story of Harry Potter from an omniscient point of view. Why do you think she did so?

3 Things to Think About

GOOD STORIES COME in all shapes and sizes and can be told in any number of ways. Some writers like to use a lot of dialogue; some use almost none. Some authors like to describe the setting of their scenes in intricate detail; some do it in a sentence or two and get on with the action. All writers have the same basic set of tools at their disposal to use in creating the best fiction they can. What follows is a breakdown of some of these tools and suggestions on how to use them to best advantage.

Point of View

Now that you've come up with a good main character and the basic beginning, middle, and end of your story, it's essential to find the right way to tell it. Should the story be narrated by the main character, as Twain has Huck do in *The Adventures of Huckleberry Finn*? Or should the writer narrate the story, as Rowling does in the Harry Potter books? There are different points of view (POV) an author can use to tell a tale. The challenge is to find the one that best suits the particular story.

The First Person

A story from the first-person POV is narrated by one of the characters. Today most literature written for teens is written in the first person. Why? For one thing, it allows the writer to tell the story in a unique voice. Take the opening sentences of Judy Blume's *Are You There God? It's Me, Margaret.*

> **We moved on the Tuesday before Labor Day. I knew what the weather was like the second I got up. I knew because I caught my mother sniffing under her arms.**

Look at how much information is conveyed in three short sentences. Right away, readers know that the story is about someone who has just moved and, by the third sentence, that this person is most probably a teenager—and one with a sense of humor who is not afraid to joke about her mother checking her armpits on a hot day.

Skillfully handled, the first person can give the reader a sharper sense of the main character. If that character is quirky, overly serious, or hilarious, it can come through in his or her own words. In the novel *High Fidelity*, Nick Hornby's use of the first person allows the main character,

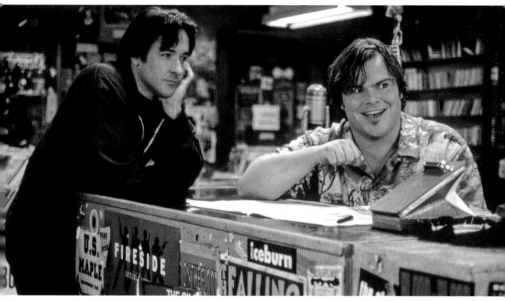

When *High Fidelity* became a movie, the screenwriter tried to retain the first person point of view, but it's impossible to have the same immediacy on screen as on the page.

Rob, to describe himself in a way that no impersonal narrator ever could.

> **My genius, if one can call it that, is to combine a whole load of averageness into one compact frame. I'd say that there were millions like me, but there aren't, really: lots of blokes have impeccable music taste but don't read, lots of blokes read but are really fat, lots of blokes are sympathetic to feminism but have stupid beards. . . .**

Notice how the first person can give a story a more casual feel, almost as though the narrator is an old friend confiding in the reader. Of course, depending on the kind of story the writer wants to tell, this more casual tone can also be a drawback. An epic adventure about good conquering evil such as *The Lord of the Rings* requires a more formal narrator who can oversee and comment upon all the action.

Another drawback to first person is quite simple. It can limit the scenes you can dramatize. If the central event of your story is a fire that strikes your narrator's home when he is at camp, it is going to be pretty hard to have him describe it. If your main character's two best friends have a conversation behind his back, again, it is going to be hard to depict. First person works best when the narrator is involved in nearly every scene. A giant novel such as Tolstoy's *War and Peace*, a book with hundreds of characters and scenes, would never work in the first person.

The Third Person

If the first person is a story narrated by one of the characters, the third person is a story in which the narrator is *not* one of the characters. Though there are different technical terms to describe different kinds of third-person POV, the most common is called "third person omniscient." This is a POV where the narrator has what has been described as a God's-eye view of the action and is able to see and describe every character, event, and emotion in the story.

The third person holds many advantages. Many stories have too many characters or take place in too many different locations for one first-person narrator to be able to see or describe (remember *War and Peace*). Authors often want the leeway (or, freedom) to be able to describe the inner life of all of their characters in the depth that a single first-person narrator wouldn't be able to accomplish. In the right hands, it is a POV that can give a story great weight. In the opening of *A Christmas Carol*, Dickens uses the third person to set the scene with sweeping authority.

> **Marley was dead, to begin with. There is no doubt whatever about that. The register of his burial was signed by the clergyman, the clerk, the undertaker, and the chief mourner. Scrooge signed it. And Scrooge's name was good upon 'Change for anything he chose to put his hand to.**
>
> **Old Marley was as dead as a doornail.**

Herman Wouk uses the third person in the opening of his novel, *City Boy: The Adventures of Herbie Bookbinder*.

> **On a golden May morning in the sixth year of Calvin Coolidge's presidency, a stout little dark-haired boy named Herbert Bookbinder, dressed in a white shirt, a blue tie and gray knee breeches, sat at a desk in Public School 50 in the Bronx, suffering the pain of a broken heart.**

The story of Scrooge and Tiny Tim is so timeless that the word *Scrooge* has made it into our vocabularies to describe someone stingy and mean.

Wouk's third-person narrator not only knows the month, year, and setting but also is able to describe the main character's looks, clothes and emotional state—and do it all with elegance and wit. Not bad for a single sentence.

So which POV should you use when you sit down to write? First, think about your story a little bit. Is it the type of tale that might work better narrated in the first person? Does your main character have an interesting voice that might enhance your story if used to narrate it? Or would the third person be better?

A good rule of thumb is to start with whatever seems most natural. When you're starting a new story, use whatever POV feels right. Remember: writing is a process of trial and error. If upon rereading, you think the story might benefit from another POV, go ahead and try it.

Dialogue

One of the best ways to let the reader get to know the characters in a story is to let them talk. Most good fiction has good dialogue. When should dialogue be used and how often? Again, it depends on the writer and the story. Jack London's famous short story *To Build a Fire*, a tale of a man walking to his doom in the arctic North, has no dialogue— just pages of vivid and dramatic description. Hemingway, on the other hand, often lets his characters talk for pages with very little interrupting description or explanation.

Does fictional dialogue model real conversation? The answer is no. Real conversations are often too messy and way too long. Speakers usually take too long to get to the

The Second Person

As in the third person, second person POV stories are told by a narrator. However, that narrator tells what *you* said and did. Used very rarely, the most famous recent example is from Jay McInerney's novel *Bright Lights, Big City*, published in 1984.

"You are not the kind of guy who would be at a place like this at this time of the morning. But here you are, and you cannot say that the terrain is entirely unfamiliar, although the details are fuzzy."

point and fill gaps with phrases such as "you know" and "whatever." For example, imagine two old friends running into each other on the first day of school. The real conversation might go something like this:

> "Hey, Tricia."
> "Charlotte."
> "So. Wow. Here we are."
> "I know."
> "School."
> "Yeah."
> "Weird, huh?"
> "When did you get back in town?"
> "A week ago." (She waves at someone else.)
> "Oh, hi Jim!" (Looks back at Tricia.)
> "I was at camp."
> "Camp? Really?"
> "Yeah. Really."
> "Cool."

Just because such a conversation might actually occur doesn't mean that it will work on the page. A fictionalized version might be reduced to something like this, using dialogue and narration:

> "Yo! Hi!"
> Glancing down the hall, Tricia sucked in
> a deep breath. She hadn't seen Charlotte

since she got back in town, and wasn't sure
she wanted to now.

"Where were you this summer?" Charlotte
said, walking toward her.

Tricia forced a smile. "Camp."

In the end, good dialogue depends upon your ability
to get real-sounding conversation down on the page. That
depends on your ear. Which means you need to listen to
people talk and think about what kinds of things your
characters might say. Are our characters uneducated but
street smart like Huck Finn? Or are they courageous men,
hobbits, dwarves, and elves engaged in epic struggles of
life and death like the characters in *The Lord of the Rings*?
Are they young or old? Happy or sad? All of these factors
will affect how characters sound.

Exposition

Now it's time to discuss exposition—that is, the background information that a reader needs to know in order
to follow the story. Good writers are able to tell their stories without the exposition feeling forced. How do they
do it? Again, it's trial and error. Sometimes it is best to
simply summarize past events for the reader. Sometimes
it's better to hold back certain information until later
in the story. (To summarize everything in the first few
pages can overwhelm a reader with information.) Some
writers use dialogue to get out needed exposition. Using

Dialogue: Three Rules

1. The spoken words go in quotation marks.

2. Place a comma after the final spoken word, before the final quotation mark. Then put the period at the end of the sentence. Exceptions: when the spoken thought is a question or an exclamation.

3. Try not to modify what your characters say with adverbs. Let the power of a scene and the strength of the characterizations tell the reader the character's emotions.

Here are some examples:

Correct: "Boy, it's hot out today," Dan said.

Not: "Boy, it's hot out today." Dan said, tiredly.

Correct: "Did you go to the fair?" Carrie asked.

Not: "Did you go to the fair," Carrie asked, hopefully?

Correct: "I love baseball!" John said.

Not: "I love baseball," John said, excitedly!

a conversation to fill in information about the plot can be clunky, however, as can be seen in the following dialogue:

> "Say," Bill said as Hal walked into his restaurant. "I haven't see you here in a while."
>
> Hal sighed. "Well, I haven't felt comfortable poking my nose around here since the murder."
>
> "Oh, yeah," Bill said, remembering. "That was two years ago, right?"
>
> "No, three," Hal said. "On July 23rd. And Stanley was my best friend, too."
>
> "I remember. I also remember the time he was sued by his mother-in-law for accidentally running over her pet hamster."

Dialogue that sums up exposition so obviously should be avoided. That doesn't mean that certain information shouldn't be revealed in dialogue. If something dramatic that affects the emotional life of a major character occurs in your story—say, your protagonist discovers that her husband is leaving her—it probably makes sense to dramatize the scene using dialogue so the reader can experience how she feels. In the end, however, working out the best way to present your scenes and reveal information to your reader is a matter of experimenting. Try it one way. If you love it, great. If not, cross it out and rewrite.

Make It Happen

What makes a good scene in a book?
The answer is simple. Good scenes
are those in which things happen to
the characters. Not every book has to
begin with a chase scene or a shoot-out,
of course. But stories need to move.
The reader needs to feel as though
the characters are on a journey—that
important things are happening to them.
If a scene in your story feels dull, ask
yourself what is happening to the main
characters in it. If the answer is "not
much," then you might want to rewrite
it in a way that has more action.

Good Writing: Strong Verbs and Choice Details

Some young writers think that to write well requires a fancy prose style that features an endless string of paragraph-long sentences. Maybe you will turn out to be a stylist who favors more florid prose. Or perhaps your natural style will be more direct. However you write, it helps to remember that it is strong verbs that give a piece of writing its punch and vitality. Fitzgerald's *The Great Gatsby* is regarded as one of the most beautifully written American novels. Notice how Fitzgerald's sentences are always rooted in strong verbs. Describing a wild party at Gatsby's house, he writes,

> **The lights grow brighter as the earth lurches away from the sun. . . .**
>
> **Suddenly one of the gypsies, in trembling opal, seizes a cocktail out of the air, dumps it down for courage and, moving her hands like Frisco, dances out alone on the canvas platform.**

The earth doesn't move away from the sun, it *lurches*. The gypsy doesn't grab a cocktail, she *seizes* it. She doesn't drink it for courage but *dumps it down*. Fitzgerald's prose is known for being highly descriptive, almost florid at times, but his sentences are rooted in rock-solid nouns and verbs.

Many believe that *The Great Gatsby* is the great American novel; most agree that it is one of the most beautifully written stories of all time.

Mark Twain once said, "When you catch an adjective, kill it"—another way of saying that good writing comes from choosing strong verbs. Still, every writer needs to describe things. For example, your story may take place in

59

a kitchen. Do you need to spend an entire page describing every detail? You can, but it's by no means necessary. A single detail—if it's the right one—can tell more about a scene than twenty bad ones. The same goes for describing a character. If you want to give the reader a mental picture of your character, go for one or two striking details (most readers like to visualize the characters in their own way). In his short story "The Things They Carried," Tim O'Brien doesn't give a straightforward physical description of the main character, Jimmy Cross. Instead, O'Brien finds a telling detail or two to give the reader a fuller, more interesting picture. The story begins:

> **First Lieutenant Jimmy Cross carried letters from a girl named Martha, a junior at Mount Sebastian College in New Jersey. . . . In the later afternoon, after a day's march, he would dig his foxhole, hold them with the tips of his fingers. . . . He would sometimes taste the envelope flaps, knowing her tongue had been there.**

O'Brien could have told us that Jimmy Cross was tall or short or even that he had been wounded by a mortar. Instead, O'Brien wrote that Jimmy would sometimes taste the envelope flaps of a girl he liked—a detail that reveals much more about Jimmy's sense of isolation and loneliness.

Whether you feel a scene or character needs a description that's long or short, search for the detail or details that make it your own. Here's how E. B. White describes Wilbur the pig's dinner in *Charlotte's Web*: "It was a delicious meal—skim milk . . . half a doughnut, the rind of a summer squash, two pieces of stale toast, a third of a gingersnap . . . and a spoonful of raspberry jello." Every detail is fresh. The toast isn't just toast—it's *stale* toast. It's not one gingersnap but a *third* of a gingersnap.

When writing, often the first detail you think of turns out to be a cliché—something the reader has heard before. Don't be so easy on yourself. Tweak your words, think of some other way to say the same thing, make your details your own. It can be difficult, but it's worth the effort. Your writing will improve immeasurably.

Writing classes can be helpful. Showing your manuscript to a teacher or a friend can be helpful, too. In the long run, though, a good writer needs to read. Turn off your TV, put down your iPod and Gameboy, and ask your English teacher, friends, parents, or librarian to recommend some good books. Pile them up and get going. You won't like everything—no one does. When you do read something you love, reread it; study the author's technique. Note how the sentences are constructed, how the characters are introduced and described, how the writer sets up a scene, how the plot works. Ray Kinsella, the author of *Shoeless Joe*, advises, "When you find something that thrills you, take it apart paragraph by paragraph, line by line, word by word, to see what made it so wonderful. Then use those tricks the next time you write."

Start Reading!

"Read, read, read. Read everything—trash, classics, good and bad, and see how they do it. Just like a carpenter who works as an apprentice and studies the master. Read! You'll absorb it. Then write. If it is good, you'll find out. If it's not, throw it out the window."

—William Faulkner

Don't hesitate to imitate the writers you admire. That is how you learn. As Gay Talese once wrote, "The 'best advice' I think is in reading good writers . . . for we learn best by emulating the best."

F. Scott Fitzgerald on Exclamation Points

"Cut out all those exclamation marks. An exclamation mark is like laughing at your own joke."

4

From Start to Finish

IT IS TIME TO WRITE. So you sit at your desk and open a blank document on your computer. After thinking for a minute or two, you find yourself checking your e-mail. Then it's time for a snack. Finally, back at the desk, you write an opening sentence. It's terrible. You cross it out and try again. The new one is even worse. So you decide to start with a line of dialogue and then angrily delete the whole thing. Time to check your e-mail again.

Sound familiar? Getting started on a new piece of writing can be very exciting but is sometimes also frustrating. The fact that you are sitting at a desk is a great start, however. (Nora Roberts, the romance writer, says the secret to writing is "Place butt in chair.") Now you have to give yourself permission to write badly.

Less Is Sometimes More

Most first drafts are too long. When rewriting, do not be scared to cut out your words—lots of words. The playwright Ben Jonson wrote, "Read over your compositions and, when you meet a passage which you think is particularly fine, strike it out."

The First Draft

Give yourself permission to write *badly*? What does that mean? Many would-be writers don't write at all because they are too critical of every word they type. But no story is perfect the first time. In her book *Bird by Bird*, Anne Lamott wrote, "People tend to look at successful writers . . . and think that they sit down at their desks every morning feeling like a million dollars . . . and dive in, typing fully formed sentences as fast as a court reporter."

Nothing could be further from the truth. Even the best writers need multiple drafts to get their stories to read the way they want them to. So one key to getting started is to embrace the fact that your first draft may not be that good. In fact, it might be terrible. But that's OK. Once you have something down on paper it's much easier to rewrite and make what's not very good a little bit better.

So, if you begin with a sentence you know is truly lousy, maybe it's better not to cross it out but to keep on going. Don't let yourself become overwhelmed by how much work is ahead of you. Don't think, "This first chapter needs to introduce my main character and her entire family, and the next needs to have a chase scene where I describe Mt. Everest even though I've never been there, and the third chapter has a character who speaks Swahili." Just take it sentence by sentence, paragraph by paragraph. Let your thoughts flow. Remember what excited you about the piece of writing in the first place. You can think about your characters all day long, but it's only through the act of getting something down on paper that you'll really get to know them. You don't have to worry about other people seeing it and laughing at you. This draft is just for you—no one else gets to see it.

The Second Draft

Congratulations! You have written a first draft. Maybe it is so bad it makes you physically ill to think about it, but that is all right. According to Stephen King, writing a novel is like "crossing the Atlantic in a bathtub." In other words, it is difficult—but because you have whipped off a first draft, you are in the water, headed out to sea.

But writers are famous for being insecure. Don't let yourself get knotted up in negative thinking. When you sit down to reread your first draft, don't think, "This is gonna suck, I'm such a loser. Who ever told me I could write anyway? My work is trash." Instead, be positive. Realize that every writer—*every writer*—starts from a draft that's less than perfect. When you reread what you've written, take note of what needs to be changed. Cross out what's no good—there might be a lot. Entire pages might get the axe. But also notice what's good and build on that.

Gustave Flaubert, the author of the great novel *Madame Bovary*, once wrote, "Prose is like hair; it shines with combing." E. B. White, the author who wrote *Charlotte's Web*, said, "The best writing is rewriting." Truer words have never been spoken. Some of the greatest authors in history rewrote their books time and again before they were published. Why should you be any different? Writing is

A Lousy First Draft

To help you see how an editor can rip into a piece of writing, I've decided to put my own work on display (please see following page). My second children's novel was *Jason and the Baseball Bear*. Here's a page from the first draft. Every typed word is mine. Every cross-out mark in pencil is from my editor. What I wrote wasn't bad. I just went on too long. If this happens to you, don't sweat it. It's normal to overwrite in a first draft—that is what they are for.

belted up his maroon Apaches uniform and

Jason /grabbed his mitt and cap and ~~after a quick sandwich, he~~
~~and his parents left their apartment for the ballfield.~~

The Munson's lived on ~~4th street~~ *Merriweather* and ~~Avenue C~~ *Meadow*, a five minute
walk from the zoo and seven and a half minutes from the ballfield.
~~The family strolled up tree-lined 4th street and turned right on~~
~~Avenue A. It was a warm, breezy day - perfect for baseball. They~~
~~entered the park at 7th street, walked down a stone pathway, and then~~
~~turned a wide corner. Before them was the ballfield.~~

Though most ~~people~~ *fans* hadn't begun to arrive, ~~the field was~~
~~beginning to buzz with activity.~~ Players were stretching on the grass,
~~and~~ warming up. The umpire was dusting off homeplate. A teenaged boy
~~was~~ pick*ed* up a few pieces of trash that had blown into the
outfield. A hotdog vendor ~~was~~ plac*ing* mustard packets in his pockets.
In rightfield, an old man was adjusting the lettering on the
scoreboard ~~to read:~~

```
              1 2 3 4 5 6 7 8 9 10 11 12  H R E
APACHES
HIGHLANDERS

         OUTS 0   BALLS 0   STRIKES  0
```

~~Jason and his parents entered the field by the left field foul~~
~~pole and walked down the left field line.~~

~~"Well, here we are," Mrs. Munson exclaimed as the family came to~~
~~a halt by third base.~~

~~"It's exciting," Dr. Munson said. "Your mother and I are very~~
~~proud of you."~~

~~"Thanks," Jason said.~~
Jason was about run onto the field when his father
~~Dr. Munson~~ squatted down next to his son.

10

a process. It begins when you gather the courage to sit in front of that blank sheet of paper or computer screen—it ends many drafts later.

> One of the few things I know about writing is this: Spend it all, shoot it, play it, lose it all, right away, every time. Do not hoard what seems good for a later place in the book, or for another book, give all, give it now.
>
> —Annie Dillard

Caring

By now you might be asking, "Multiple drafts? How am I going to do that?"

The answer is in the most important writing rule of them all. To give a piece of writing the time, effort, and love it requires, you must care about it deeply. Sound obvious? Well, lots of writers—even talented ones—sometimes make the mistake of pursuing a story or subject that doesn't truly excite them. So if you're feeling frustrated, try to avoid negative thinking: "I stink. Let me drop creative writing and take advanced calculus instead." The problem probably isn't that you have no talent. It's that you have the wrong subject.

That subject could be anything. My first novel, *The Worldwide Dessert Contest*, is about a man who desperately wants to win a dessert contest with the world's largest apple pancake. In a more serious vein, Tim O'Brien finds his inspiration in the Vietnam War. Paul Auster likes to write strange tales set in Brooklyn, New York. Whatever your subject, you have to feel inspired by it. If you aren't, then it's unlikely that anyone else will be. Joyce Carol Oates said, "Any writer who has difficulty in writing is probably not onto his true subject . . . as soon as you connect with your true subject you will write."

So keep looking. Writing is partly about talent, but it is more about hard work. All successful writers have had moments of doubt—some have even had teachers and editors tell them to give up. But they kept on going until they found the subject that made their work come alive. As the playwright Samuel Beckett once said, "Ever failed? No matter. Try again. Fail again. Fail better."

Born Too Short— a Novel from Start to Finish

Like most pieces of writing, my book, *Born Too Short: The Confessions of an 8th Grade Basket Case*, needed lots of rewriting along the way. The book tells the comic but true-to-life tale of Matt Greene, a likable but unextraordinary eighth grader at the Hannaford School in New York City. Matt's best friend is Keith Livingston, a boy who not only is the best-looking kid in the grade but is also tall and blond and, as Matt puts it, "has made out with more girls than I have toes." As the plot thickens, Matt becomes so jealous that he makes a wish that Keith's life fall apart. To his horror, it happens! Of course, there is no such thing as magic—at least not in this book—so Keith is merely experiencing life's usual ups and downs. It takes a while for Matt to figure that out.

So, that is the basic story. Here's a break-down of how I got started.

1996: I had the germ of the idea: a story about the lousy feeling everyone has at one time or another: being jealous of a good friend.

1997: I wrote a screenplay about a thirty-year-old guy in New York City who becomes so jealous of his four best friends that he wishes that their lives would fall apart. I called it *Green*.

1998: The screenplay did not sell. I put it in my drawer to collect dust.

1999: I worked on other projects. The screenplay continued to collect dust. Mold, too.

2000: Looking for a new project, I remembered my old screenplay. Maybe it would work as a young-adult novel told in the first person by a humorously tortured teenage boy who was a little bit on the short, unathletic side?

2001 (winter): I wrote a few chapters. An editor I had worked with in the past liked them. I wrote some more. That summer I finished my first draft. The main character, now named Matt, was jealous of his two best friends.

2001 (spring): Unfortunately, Matt's two best friends weren't coming into sharp enough focus. After a week or two of despair, I realized that the novel would be better if Matt were jealous of only one friend, Keith. Once I made that decision, the story began to gel.

2001 (spring, summer, fall): I wrote draft after draft. Lots of scenes were cut; others were rewritten. When I finally finished, I had to find a good title. I tried many: *Me and the Guy with the Movie Star Gums*; *Greene with Envy*; *Second Banana*; *Hating Keith*; *Tall Story from a Short Hero*; *I Can Laugh about It Now*; *Single White Short Guy*; *Promise Not to Hate Me*; *Confessions of a Lip-sucking God*. *Born Too Short*, I decided finally, seemed to sum up the plight of the main character—

a funny take on a guy who feels the pain of feeling less than lovable.

From *Born Too Short*:

By the time the party was over, and I hit the pavement with Derrick, all my bottled-up feelings—feelings that had been building for most of a year—began to spill out. And I mean spill. Then, on the corner of 81st and Columbus Avenue I sort of snapped. I mean, REALLY SNAPPED. All the jealousy, envy, and anger that had been festering in my guts thundered out of me like I was possessed. It was freaky.

"You know what'd make me happy?" I shouted. "If for just once Keith'd suck at every sport!"

—Dan Elish

Your Reward

With all this rewriting, it might be fair to ask, "How does the writer know when it's finished?" Some swear by an old adage: "A piece of writing is never finished, it's abandoned." There is some truth to that. A writer can always find something to change, a sentence to cut, or a detail to tweak.

Still, there comes a moment when it's time to stop—a time when you feel you've given the piece all you can. At that point, it's finally time to share your work with a friend, parent, or teacher. If you're taking a creative writing class, you can present it there. But be careful. Different

You've labored and labored so long it's hard to judge the quality of your work—now's the time to share it with a group of trusted peers.

people have different taste. If someone says your story is terrible, it might have to do with how he or she is feeling that day. Maybe the person who read your manuscript just got cut from the basketball team. Maybe you gave your work to someone who hates reading.

So make sure that you respect whoever is critiquing you. Even then, get several different opinions and ask your critics to back up their opinions. If someone you trust makes a good point, be open to doing some more rewriting. Never forget: it is *your* story. If you disagree, it's all right to keep it the way it is.

After you've given your story a final polish, it's time for publication. I'm not talking about professionally (there's time for that later if you get serious about your work), but how about submitting your work to your school literary magazine? Don't be shy. People won't expect you to be another Mark Twain or Stephenie Meyer right off the bat. Now that you've done the hard work of putting words on paper, share them with the world. Whether the response is positive or negative, remember that writing's greatest joys have little to do with other people's opinions of your work. In the end, writing's satisfaction has to do with expressing yourself with words that are yours and yours alone. With a few sentences you can create a new world and lead your readers into a fresh "fictional dream." To do it well is hard but far from impossible. The opportunity to sit down every day and try is writing's greatest reward.

Writing Tips

1. Been sitting at your computer too long? Stuck? Take a walk, ride a bike, or go for a jog. You'll be surprised how writing problems get resolved while on a break. Exercise clears the mind.

2. Having trouble getting started in the morning? Read through what you wrote the day before; edit your writing as you go. By the time you get to where you left off, you'll be warmed up.

3. Be prepared—ideas come at the strangest times and places. Some writers carry around a pen and paper to jot down good ideas as they come.

En route to a finished piece, every writer has to learn to cut and edit. It can be hard, but it's worth it!

5 Writing Exercises

SOME PEOPLE HATE WRITING EXERCISES, preferring to jump right in with their own stories. For those writers who get stuck, here are some fun exercises that might help you get started.

1. Write a story that includes three strange details. For example, write a short story that includes a purple pickle, a pink ping-pong ball, and a Bermuda onion.

2. Write the first paragraph of your story in the third person. Now write it in the first person from the perspective of your main character. Now write it in the first person from the POV of another character, then another. This fun exercise might help you learn a thing or two about your characters.

3. Take one of your favorite novels off the shelf. Type out your favorite passages, studying the use of language as you go.

4. Do you feel that your characters seem two-dimensional, or lacking in depth? Write a paragraph about each character's background; include the character's hometown, his or her likes and dislikes, and where he or she went to school. You never know what you will discover that may be useful.

5. Write a paragraph using only one-syllable words. This exercise will focus your attention on the choice of each word.

6. Take a picture that is important to you, such as your parents' wedding photo, and use it as the jump-off point to a one-page story.

7. Write a story about your pet. Now write a story about a pet that you've never owned.

8. Write five different opening sentences for the same story. Which one tells the reader more about the setting and characters? Which one draws the reader in?

Introduction

p. 6, "Everybody is talented . . .": Jon Winokur, *Advice to Writers*, New York: Vintage, 1999, 44.

Chapter One

pp. 13–14, "It is a truth universally . . .": Jane Austen, *The Complete Novels of Jane Austen*, New York: Vintage, 1976, 279.

p. 14, "It was the best of times . . .": Charles Dickens, *A Tale of Two Cities*, New York: CreateSpace, 2009, 3.

p. 16, "It is scarcely conceivable . . .": Harriet Martineau, *A Brief History of the Novel*, www.docstoc.com/docs/2186248/A-BRIEF-HISTORY-OF-THE-NOVEL, chapter 29, PowerPoint presentation.

p. 16, "A boy's story is the . . .": Brainy Media.com, "Brainy Quote," www.brainyquote.com/quotes/authors/c/charles_dickens.html.

p. 17, "No Victorian novel approaches . . .": V. S. Pritchett, *The Living Novel and Later Appreciations*, New York: Random House, 1947, 101–102.

Fiction

p. 20, "You don't know about me . . .": Mark Twain, *The Adventures of Huckleberry Finn*, New York: Pocket Books, 1971, 1.

p. 23, "Most of the big shore places were . . .": F. Scott Fitzgerald, *The Great Gatsby*, chapter 9, http://ebooks. adelaide.edu.au/f/fitzgerald/f_scott/gatsby/.

p. 25, "A short story must have a single mood . . .": Jon Winokur, *Advice to Writers*, New York: Vintage Books, 1999, 57.

p. 27, "If you want to be a writer, you can . . .": Winokur, *Advice to Writers*, 44.

Chapter Two

p. 30, "I would never write about . . .": Jon Winokur, *Advice to Writers*, New York: Vintage Books, 1999, 9.

p. 32, "Writing a novel is a very hard thing . . .": Winokur, *Advice to Writers*, 45.

pp. 34–35, "Find out what your hero or heroine wants . . .": Winokur, *Advice to Writers*, 172.

p. 35, "Nothing is as important as . . .": Winokur, *Advice to Writers*, 7.

p. 39, "Plot grows out of character . . .": Winokur, *Advice to Writers*, 96.

p. 41, "I have never demanded of a set . . .": Stephen King, *On Writing*, New York: Pocket Books, 2000, 161.

p. 43, "We read five words on the first page . . .": John Gardner, *On Becoming a Novelist*, New York: Harper & Row, 1983, 5.

Chapter Three

p. 46, "We moved on the Tuesday before Labor Day . . .": Judy Blume, *Are You There God? It's Me, Margaret*, New York: Dell, 1970, 1.

p. 47, "My genius, if one can call it that . . .": Nick Hornby, *High Fidelity*, London: Gollancz, 1995, 30.

p. 49, "Marley was dead, to begin with . . .": Charles Dickens, *A Christmas Carol*, New York: Scholastic, 1962, 1.

p. 49, "On a golden May morning in the sixth year . . .": Herman Wouk, *City Boy: The Adventures of Herbie Bookbinder*, Boston: Little Brown, 1992, 1.

p. 52, "You are not the kind of guy who would be . . .": Jay McInerney, *Bright Lights, Big City*, New York: Vintage, 1984, 1.

p. 58, "The lights grow brighter as the earth . . .": Fitzgerald, *The Great Gatsby*, chapter 3, http://ebooks.adelaide.edu.au/f/fitzgerald/f_scott/gatsby/.

p. 59, "When you catch an adjective, kill it . . .": Jon Winokur, *Advice to Writers*, New York: Vintage Books, 1999, 75.

p. 60, "First Lieutenant Jimmy Cross carried letters . . .": Tim O'Brien, *The Things They Carried*, Boston: Houghton Mifflin, 1990, 3.

p. 61, "It was a delicious meal—skim milk . . .": E. B. White, *Charlotte's Web*, New York: Harper & Row, 1952, 75.

p. 61, "When you find something that . . .": Winokur, *Advice to Writers*, 139.

p. 62, "Read, read, read. Read everything—trash, classics . . .": Winokur, *Advice to Writers*, 139.

Fiction

p. 63, "The 'best advice' I think is in reading good writers . . .": Winokur, *Advice to Writers*, 205.

p. 63, "Cut out all those exclamation marks . . .": Winokur, *Advice to Writers*, 121.

Chapter Four

p. 66, "Read over your compositions . . .": Jon Winokur, *Advice to Writers*, New York: Vintage Books, 1999, 168.

p. 67, "People tend to look at successful writers . . .": Anne Lamott, *Bird by Bird*, New York, Random House, 1994, 21.

p. 68, "crossing the Atlantic in a bathtub . . .": Stephen King, *On Writing*, New York: Pocket Books, 2000, 210.

p. 68, "Prose is like hair . . .": Winokur, *Advice to Writers*, 105.

p. 68, "The best writing is rewriting . . .": Winokur, *Advice to Writers*, 105.

p. 71, "One of the few things I know about writing is this . . .": Winokur, *Advice to Writers*, 48.

p. 72, "Any writer who has difficulty in writing . . .": Winokur, *Advice to Writers*, 196.

p. 72, "Ever failed? No matter . . .": Winokur, *Advice to Writers*, 52.

p. 76, "By the time the party was over, and I hit the pavement . . .": Dan Elish, *Born Too Short: The Confessions of an Eighth-Grade Basket Case*, New York: Simon Pulse, 2002, 58.

All websites were accessible and accurate as of August 31, 2010.

Further Information

Books

Ellis, Sherry. *Now Write!* New York: Penguin, 2006.

Huddle, David. *The Writing Habit: Essays*. Salt Lake City: Peregrine Smith Books, 1991.

King, Stephen. *On Writing*. New York: Pocket Books, 2000.

Lamott, Anne. *Bird by Bird*. New York, Random House, 1994.

Fiction

Websites

Daily Writing Tips

www.dailywritingtips.com/creative-writing-101/

Story Writing Tips for Kids

www.coreygreen.com/storytips.html

All websites were accurate and accessible as of August 31, 2010.

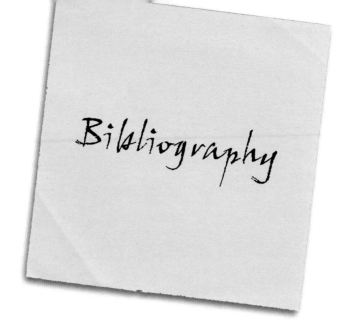

Bibliography

Gardner, John. *On Becoming a Novelist*. New York: Harper & Row, 1983.

Gotham Writers' Workshop. *Writing Fiction*. New York: Bloomsbury, 2003.

Huddle, David. *The Writing Habit: Essays*. Salt Lake City: Peregrine Smith Books, 1991.

King, Stephen. *On Writing*. New York: Pocket Books, 2000.

Lamott, Anne. *Bird by Bird*. New York: Random House, 1994.

Winokur, Jon. *Advice to Writers*. New York: Vintage Books, 1999.

Index

Page numbers in **boldface** are illustrations. Proper names of fictional characters, and fictional places, are shown by (C).

Fiction

Fiction

About the Author

DAN ELISH is the author of numerous novels for readers of all ages, including *The Misadventures of Justin Hearnfeld*, *The Attack of the Frozen Woodchucks*, and *Born Too Short*, a young adult choice for the International Reading Association in 2004. Dan has also written many nonfiction titles for Marshall Cavendish Benchmark and was the co-writer of the book for the Broadway musical, *13*. He lives in New York City with his wife and two children.